SRI LANKA

Text by
Rohan Gunaratna

B
BONECHI

INDEX

We wish to thank Jennifer Henricus, Executive Editor, Meeting Point Inc., Chandra Subasinghe, Managing Director Tapobrane Bookshop and Dr. Roland Silva, Director General, UNESCO-Sri Lanka Project of the Cultural Triangle, for their assistance in the preparation of this book.

ISBN 978-88-8029-239-5

* * *

INTRODUCTION

"Serendipity" - the discovery of beauty by coincidence or accident - is a term coined from "Serendip", the name bequeathed by seafaring Greeks to the Indian Ocean island of Sri Lanka. Two thousand years later, Sri Lanka still offers serendipity to the traveller - a rare combination of unexpected pleasures. Strikingly beautiful landscapes, unspoilt golden beaches, an abundance of marine and terrestrial wildlife combined with historic temples, gigantic monuments, and a unique culture and exquisite pageantry to make Sri Lanka a matchless tourist destination in the Orient.

The pleasure of touring Sri Lanka is heightened because one does not have to travel great distances to experience the island's many attractions. A five-hour journey by road will take the visitor from sunny beaches to the salubrious hills, or from a tropical wildlife park to the cool climes of Adam's Peak.

The serendipitous beauty of Sri Lanka is enhanced and enriched by the warm hospitality of its people. From time immemorial, the sincere smiles and warm charm of Sri Lankans have welcomed visitors from all corners of the globe.

Sri Lanka portrays what the Orient gave to the world at the turn of the Christian era - the concept of society; the birth of all the major religions; the origin of commercial and political ties; and the refinement of arts from architecture to music.

While envoys of ancient Sri Lankan kings visited Rome, Persia, China, and Egypt, visitors to Sri Lanka included Fa Hsien, the pilgrim, Marco Polo, the traveller, Ibn Battuta, the seafarer, and Robert Knox, the chronicler. They left fascinating descriptions of the island. Eighty different names, from Taprobana to Seylan and Dharmadvipa, confirm the waves of visitors that Sri Lanka attracted during its history.

The European maritime powers - the Portuguese, the Dutch and the British - who traversed the Indian Ocean from the 15th century on left indomitable marks on the island.

After five centuries of colonial domination, Sri Lanka became independent in 1948 and a republic in 1972. The country has an interesting ethnic mixture, comprising 74% Sinhalese, 12.6% Tamil, 5.5% Indian Tamil, 7.1% Moor and 0.3% Malay (Muslims), 0.3% Burgher (of European origin), and 0.3% others.

All four major religions are represented with 69% Buddhists, 15.5% Hindus, 7.5% Christians, and 7.9% Muslims.

History and legend, monuments and memorials, temples and processions, myth and folklore, fable and parable, philosophy and religion, statecraft and the art of war, and morals and the romance of modern Sri Lanka reveal the story of a new nation at crossroads - the death of an old civilization and a new culture struggling to be born.

The old amidst the new: the Lighthouse Clock Tower, at a busy road intersection in Fort Colombo, was built in to a design by Lady Ward, the wife of British Governor Sir Henry Ward.

The pink colonial façade now houses Colombo's World Trade Centre.

Page 7: pretty 19th-century buildings grace the hub of Colombo's business district.

COLOMBO

Colombo, the capital of Sri Lanka, brings together the old and the new. Colonial ruins and buildings contrast with high- rise hotels and commercial banks. Almost everyone who visits Sri Lanka spends time in this busy city. Colombo, an eighth-century port, houses administrative, financial and other offices of relevance to the traveller. A part of Colombo re-lives its past by preserving some of the finest structures of its colonial heritage. The city has developed, through several phases, into a modern city. The populace of Colombo is representative of Sri Lanka's ethnic and religious mixture.

Fort, where the Portuguese and the Dutch had their well-protected bastions during the 16th and 17th centuries, has government offices, departmental stores and shopping complexes.

The Laksala, a state-owned handicraft centre near the Millers and Cargills departmental stores on York Street, offers Sri Lankan handicrafts at fixed prices.

The Immigration and Emigration department, the Tourist Information Bureau, the General Post Office and the Airline offices are centrally located in the Fort. The Pettah, i.e. the area outside the Fort, is the busiest and noisiest part of the city, teeming with wholesale and retail outlets and wayside eateries, as well as the main railway station and public transport stands. The bustling street market known as the World Market, on Duke Street, offers clothing and leather wear at bargain prices.

Colombo's hotels are centrally located, offering the visitor both pleasure and convenience. The Galle Face Hotel and the Hotel Taj Samudra open out to the ocean and to the breezy Galle Face green where horse racing was once common. The green is popular with morning joggers and evening strollers, as well as with kite-flying enthusiasts and courting

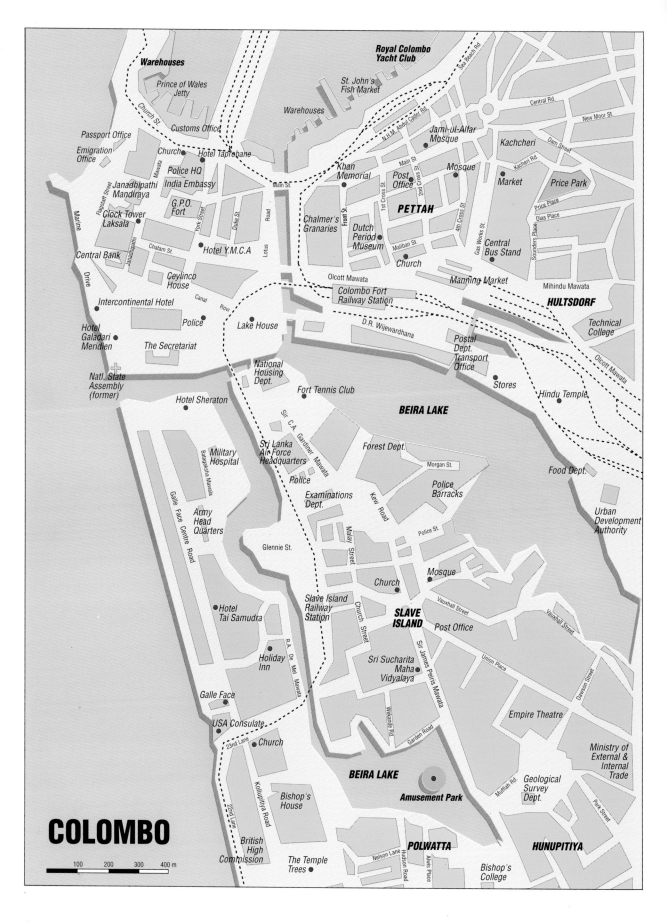

Warehouses

Royal Colombo
Yacht Club

Prince of Wales
Jetty

St. John's
Fish Market

Sea Beach Rd.

Central Rd.

New Moor St.

Church St.

Warehouses

N.H.M. Abdul Cader Rd.

Jami-ul-Alfar
Mosque

Kachcheri

Dam Street

Passport Office

Customs Office

Main St.

Mosque

Kacheri Rd.

Emigration
Office

Church

Hotel Taprobane

Khan
Memorial

Post
Office

Market

Price Park

Mawata

Police HQ

Main St

2nd Cross St

Flagstaff Street

Janadhipathi
Mandiraya

India Embassy

G.P.O.
Fort

Chalmer's
Granaries

1st Cross St

Dutch
Period
Museum

4th Cross St

PETTAH

Gas Works Rd.

Central
Bus Stand

Price Place

Dias Place

Sounders Place

York Street

Duke St.

Front St.

Clock Tower
Laksala

Janadhipathi

Chatam St.

Lotus

Road

Maliban St.

Church

Mihindu Mawata

Central Bank

Hotel Y.M.C.A

Olcott Mawata

Manning Market

HULTSDORF

Ceylinco
House

Canal

Row

Colombo Fort
Railway Station

D.R. Wijewardhana

Technical
College

Intercontinental Hotel

Lake House

Postal
Dept.
Transport
Office

Olcott Mawata

Police

Hotel
Galadari
Meridien

The Secretariat

National
Housing
Dept.

Fort Tennis Club

Stores

Hindu Temple

Natl. State
Assembly
(former)

Hotel Sheraton

Sir C.A. Gardiner Mawata

BEIRA LAKE

Forest Dept.

Food Dept.

Military
Hospital

Sri Lanka
Air Force
Headquarters

Morgan St.

Police

Police
Barracks

Urban
Development
Authority

Galle Face Centre Road

Balapaksha Mawata

Examinations
Dept.

Kew Road

Glennie St.

Malay Street

Police St.

Army
Head
Quarters

Mosque

Hotel
Tai Samudra

Church

SLAVE
ISLAND

Vauxhall Street

Vauxhall Street

R.A. De Mel Mawata

Slave Island
Railway
Station

Church Street

Post Office

Union Place

Dawson Street

Holiday
Inn

Sri Sucharita
Maha
Vidyalaya

Sir James Petris Mawata

Galle Face

USA Consulate

Empire Theatre

23rd Lane

Church

Wekande Rd.

Garden Road

Ministry of
External &
Internal
Trade

22nd Lane

Kollupitiya Road

Bishop's
House

BEIRA LAKE

Amusement Park

Muttiah Rd.

Geological
Survey
Dept.

Park Street

COLOMBO

British
High
Commission

The Temple
Trees

POLWATTA

Nelson Lane

Hudson Road

Alwis Place

HUNUPITIYA

Bishop's
College

| 100 | 200 | 300 | 400 m |

Colombo offers the visitor a choice of star-class hotels with spectacular views of the Indian Ocean and the surprise of green- clad vistas broken by neatly-tiled roofs interspersed with Buddhist temples, Christian churches and a sprinkling of mosques and Hindu temples.

couples. The old Parliament Building, a landmark on Galle Face, now accomodates the Presidential Secretariat. The President's residence is in the renovated and refurbished Governor's House, which was originally a Dutch brewery. The Colombo Renaissance Hotel is on the banks of the Beira lake, where crocodiles laze and boating is popular, while the Hotel Taprobane offers the best view of the harbour. Other conveniently-located star-class hotels are the Marriot, the Lanka Oberoi and the Intercontinental.

Colombo's oldest hotel, the Galle Face Hotel, built in the 19th century.

Road leading to Colombo through Slave Island, where the Dutch imprisoned their slaves.

The National Museum, established in 1877, is home to a unique collection depicting Sri Lanka's culture and history from prehistoric times to the present.

The roads to and from the heart of Colombo are many. On Mondays and Fridays, particularly during the rush hours when a million commuters arrive in and leave Colombo, city traffic moves slowly. Taxis and three-wheelers are the fastest conveyances, while public and private buses offer fairly good service.

The National Museum, established by the British Governor Sir William Gregory, the father of the cultural revival during the British period, was built by a descendant of a Moor, Arasy Marikar Wapuche Marikar, famous for his buildings in Grenada and Cordova. Gregory's statue adorns the lawn. For the traveller who has no time to visit historic cities, the National Museum is the best place to go to comprehend the island's past. The Archaeological Department and the Sinhala Dictionary Office are in front, and the Natural History Museum is located behind the National Museum. The buildings housing the Public Library, the National Archives and the Royal Asiatic Society, all repositories of history, are nearby.

The John de Silva Memorial Theatre, the National Art Gallery and Lionel Wendt Art Centre and Theatre, are in the vicinity.

The Department of National Museums and the Archaeological Department manage several museums in historic cities, including Ampara, Anuradhapura, Dedigama, Jaffna, Kandy, Polonnaruwa, Sigiriya and Trincomalee.

11

Some exhibits at the National Museum:
Dancing Siva, a Hindu deity.

Limestone Buddha image from Anuradhapura dating
between 300 A.D. and 500 A.D.

Wooden image of standing Buddha with a flame
over his head and a wavy 'robeline' characteristic
of the Kandyan period.

NATIONAL MUSEUM

The National Museum, a repository of Sri Lankan
art and antiques, has some of the finest bronzes,
wooden carvings and sculptures of the
Anuradhapura, Polonnaruwa and later periods.
These images are symbolic of the Sri Lankan art,
that has retained a particular tradition and distinc-
tiveness through its 2500-year-old history. The
Buddha image from Anuradhapura placed at the
entrance to the museum conforms to the classical.
The facial expression is neutral, showing an absence
of expressed feelings, but is the embodiment of
supreme wisdom and boundless compassion. The
focus of the eyes is directed at a point immediately
in front of the figure, which is characteristic of a
person in Samadhi (deep meditation).

Nandi, the vehicle of Siva.

It is not unusual to find Buddha images and Hindu images together, even in a Buddhist temple. The Polonnaruwa period was symbolic of the infusion of Hinduism into Buddhism, especially with the Sinhalese kings marrying Hindu princesses from South India. Lastly, many Buddhist temples had Hindu gods and goddesses. The sacred pantheon of Hindu gods and goddesses, mostly 12th-century bronzes from Polonnaruwa, adorn the bronze room at the museum. The bronze of Siva and Parvathi, the husband and wife combination of a family of gods and goddesses, is in a particular combination known as Umasahithamoorthy. The fire gilt image of the Buddha of the Kandyan period, found in Danagirigala Vihara in Kegalle, dates between the 17th and 19th centuries A.D.

Siva and Parvathi.

A 12th-century bronze image of a disciple of Siva Sundaramoorthi Swami; right is the image of Avalokiteswara Bodhisatva, which depicts a previous life of the Buddha characterized by princely attire. Below, seated Buddha characteristic of the Kandyan period.

14

The goddess Tara, the consort of
Bodhisatva, is a copy of the original in
the British Museum, taken from
Trincomalee in 1830. She is the
embodiment of love, compassion and
mercy. When the national treasures
were moved to Wales during World
War II, British historians categorized
this original treasure as among the
hundred best objects. The image
was insured for US $ 5.1 million
when the original was moved,
for an exhibition of the
UNESCO-Sri Lanka project
of the Cultural Triangle,
to the Commonwealth Institute
in London in 1981.

Throne and crown of the last Sri-Lankan king, Sri Wickrama Rajasinghe.

Wooden mask used in dances to exorcise devils.

Dahaatta Sanniya, or the "Eighteen Diseases", corresponding to the 18 masks depicting the 18 demons. In this healing system, those forces led by the Mahakola Sanni Yaka, the leader of the Sanni demons, are brought on stage and made to vow to leave the sick and thereby to cure the ailment.

The regalia of Sri Wickrama Rajasinghe is among the treasures of kings and queens displayed in the museum. The throne, kept at Windsor Castle in England during the British rule of the island, was used by Queen Victoria before being returned to Sri Lanka by British royalty.

The use of masks has its origins in folk rituals and in pre-

Buddhist culture. Wooden masks worn to exorcise devils during religious ceremonies, in processions and in dance and drama, are preserved in the museum. Many of these ancient rituals, practiced even now, have become the subject of intense study by scholars and scientists interested in the psychoso-matic aspects of treatment. The mask of a mythical bird, cited in folklore, is depicted as a dreadful Raksha or Demon in the Kolam dance. These masks are reproduced for the traveller to Sri Lanka in Ambalangoda, a coastal town best known for its mask carving.

THE NATIONAL ZOOLOGICAL GARDENS

The National Zoological Gardens in Dehlwala are one of the best zoos in Asia. A comprehensive collection of birds, fish, mammals and snakes, many species indigenous only to Sri Lanka, is the key attraction. The conservation programmes for the Gardens are complemented by educational and scientific programmes designed to enhance the knowledge of the public as well as of the specialists.

Hippopotamus, left, and Elephant Dances at the famous Zoological Gardens at Dehiwala, two miles south of Colombo.

Typical Sri-Lankan architecture carried over from the early colonial period.

Buddhist Simamalaka temple on Beira lake in Colombo.

*The Isurumuniya rock temple in Anuradhapura, built in
the 3rd century B.C.*

ANURADHAPURA

The citadel of Anuradhapura, the first capital founded by King Pandukabhaya and the seat of government for centuries, is symbolic of the golden era of Sri Lanka.

The island's history starts with the legendary migration of Prince Vijaya and his followers from North India five centuries before the birth of Christ. Vijaya was succeeded by Upatissa, Panduvasudeva, Abhaya, Pandukabhaya, Mutasiva and Devanampiyatissa.

Buddhism was introduced to Sri Lanka during the reign of King Devanampiyatissa, in the 3rd century B.C. Even though Anuradhapura was abandoned as the political capital following the South Indian inva-

sions, the Bo tree continued to be worshipped.

Isurumuniya houses a collection of high-relief sculptures of the 8th century consisting of laughing lions, both at the site and at the pleasure gardens: the relaxed posture of a deity is identified by some as Parjana and by others as Iyanar.

Religious and secular art and architecture, carvings and sculpture, paintings and inscriptions, have survived the elements for over 15 centuries, enabling the traveller to fathom the glory of Anuradhapura during that period. The moonstone, which constitutes the first step to any building or shrine, is to a large extent unique to Sri Lanka, especially the decorated type. A message of welcome to the visitor

from the four quarters is enshrined in the semicircle of the four animals. Various other types of symbolism have been attributed by art historians to this impressive entrance. In communicating religious history, every Buddhist image is symbolic of a specific aspect of the master's teachings or an event in the master's life.

Some exhibits at the Isurumuniya Archaeological Museum in Anuradhapura. Left, the famous rock carving known as the Isurumuniya Lovers.

The Dakkhina Stupa is the central edifice of a monastic establishment dating back to pre-Christian times. This stupa is believed to have been erected to mark the site of King Duttagamunu's cremation. The Sinhala warrior King responsible for driving away the South Indian Tamil invaders after many heroic wars, re-established Anuradhapura as the capital of Sri Lanka. Thereafter, the King, who was committed to the propagation of Buddhism, built some of the finest monuments, which have withstood the elements and time.

The Dakkhina stupa, believed to have been built over the cremated ashes of King Dutugemunu in the 2nd century B.C.

The Sri Maha Bodhi, or sacred Bo tree (Ficus religiosa), is the oldest recorded tree in the world, and was brought to Sri Lanka from India by Princess Sanghamitta, a Buddhist nun. The tree is a sapling of the Bo tree in Budda Gaya in India under which Prince Siddhartha attained Buddhahood. Buddhists throughout the world respect the Bo tree as a living relic and as a symbol of gratitude for having provided shade for Prince Siddhartha in order for him to attain enlightenment. Today, the Sri Maha Bodhi is the most venerated of the eight religious sites in Anuradhapura. The others are the Brazen Palace, the Ruwanweliseya, the Thuparama, the Jethavana, the Abhayagiri, the Lankarama and the Mirisaweti.

Sri Maha Bodhi, the sacred Bo tree, is the oldest tree on earth and was a sapling of the tree beneath which the Buddha attained enlightenment.

Ruins of the Brazen Palace, or Loha Prasada, a residence for monks adjacent to the sacred Bo tree, which was built originally by King Dutugemunu.
The roof of the nine-storey building was covered with copper plates hence its name.

What remains of the Brazen Palace, built in the 3rd century B.C., are the 1,800 columns which once supported the nine-storey structure. Before it was destroyed by fire, the palace had 1,000 chambers, gem-studded walls, balconies and windows railed with coral, and an inner pavilion with trellises of garlands of pearls. The roof of the palace was covered with copper plates, a feature discovered recently with the unearthing of copper tiles during excavations.

The elephant wall surrounding the Ruwanweliseya.

Images and paintings adorn the relatively newly constructed shrine near the Ruwanweliseya.

Ruwanweliseya, or the "Great Stupa", is regarded as the most important of the stupas at Anuradhapura.

Ruwanweliseya, standing at 300 feet, is the oldest but smallest of the three giant edifices in brick in the world. The stupa, decorated with coral brought from the Mediterranean by an envoy of the Sri Lankan king who had an audience with the Roman Emperor Caesar Augustus, was restored by successive rulers. The stupa, built by King Duttugamunu, is surrounded by an elephant wall, a restored design of an earlier expression. The design has been repeated in Thailand, Burma, and other countries in the East where Buddhism was taught by priests from Sri Lanka. The shrine room in the courtyard of the stupa has standing Buddhas from the 8th century which have been repaired and renovated from time to time.

*Moonstones, guard stones and a forest of stone columns
bear testimony to the great civilization which flourished in
Anuradhapura until the 10th century A.D.*

What remains of many of the structures of the
Anuradhapura period are brick edifices and stone
carvings. The traveller can only imagine the wood-
en and other perishable structures which would
have given the constructions of that period beauty
and elegance. The guard stones and the moonstones
at the entrances to these structures remind the visitor of the traditions of that day. The ruins also provide an insight into the livelihoods of early Sri
Lankans, from methods of agriculture to trading
contacts and the link between the ruler and religion.
A guide to the development of the Anuradhapura
civilization - its representative art, architecture and
artifacts through 1,500 years, now preserved in the
main Archeological Museum - will help the traveller
to understand its chronology.

THE MOONSTONE

The moonstone is one of the most widespread architectural characteristics in Sri Lanka. It is in the shape
of a half-moon and is found at the base of a short
staircase, the steps of which are flanked by two
balustrades which terminate below with two enor-
mous vertical stones (guardstones).

Thuparama, the oldest stupa in Sri Lanka, is believed to enshrine the Collarbone Relic of the Buddha sent from India by Emperor Ashoka after Anuradhapura converted to Buddhism.

Over the centuries, the decorations of the moonstone have continued to be enriched and to become more elaborate. The first outer band is formed of tongues of fire which symbolize material desires. The bas-reliefs of the subsequent band are a symbolic interpretation of what Buddhism considers to be the four phases of the vital process: the depiction of the elephant symbolizes birth; the bull is the symbol of old age; the lion symbolizes disease; the horse is the symbol of death. There follows a band with steles, without flowers.

The geese which appear with a lotus flower in their beaks in the fourth band represent the illuminated person: he who abandons his home and family affections in order to search for Nirvana. In the centre there is always a half lotus, which represents the culmination of desires.

The moonstones stood at the entrance to the temple as a moment of purification for the faithful.

The Thuparama stupa, built by King Devanampiyatissa, enshrines the sacred collar bone of the Buddha. This relic, a gift from India, stands testimony to the cordial relations enjoyed by the then Sri Lankan ruler. The columns around the stupa were a part of the colonnade that supported a roof which covered the sacred edifice. Aesthetically, the interior of such a structure must have been the stunning expression of wood engineering and of the most skilful craftmanship. The edifice's conical design, unique in the architectural history of the world, continues to be discussed and debated by scholars and scientists.

The discovery of medical texts and surgical instruments dating back to the Anuradhapur period confirms the quality of life during that era. The tradition of using stone troughs as medicinal baths to cure the sick was in vogue during the Anuradhapura and subsequent Polonnaruwa periods. The patient, whether paralytic or in a coma after a snake bite, was immersed in a bath enriched with the appropriate medicinal potions that would gradually be absorbed into the body. Interestingly, the shape of the vessel was moulded to economize on the expensive fluid.

Stone trough used as medicinal bath to cure the sick during the Anuradhapura period.

*Abhayagiri stupa, left, and what remains of the
Abhayagiri monastery, above: built in 88 B.C. it was one
of the largest religious institutions in the world.*

*The moonstone at the entrance to the Abhayagiri
monastery is considered the finest in the country.*

The Abhayagiri stupa, the central ritual monument
of the Abhayagiri monastery, had a height of 375
feet and a diameter of 360 feet.
The monastery had 5,000 monks in residence. What
remains today of the monastery, established by
King Vattagamini Abhaya in 88 B.C., are only the
stone and the brick structures. The chronicle, the
Mahawamsa, as well as Chinese writings, both refer
to this monastery and tell that branches were established in Burma, and that contacts were maintained
with the Mahayana and Tantrayana monasteries of
China, Indonesia, Thailand, Burma and India.

The Samadhi Buddha, a 3rd-century A.D. image, is the sculpting of a genius. The image has broad shoulders and a lion-like expression that depicts neither happiness nor sorrow, but reflects a contemplative disposition - a prerequisite for meditation. Its serenity has been spoken of by many, including the Indian Prime Minister Jawaharlal Nehru, who claimed that he found solace while in British custody from meditating on a photograph of this image.

The Jethawana stupa, the central ritual monument of the Jethawana monastery, had a diameter of 370 feet. Established in the 3rd century A.D., the monastery was the residence of 3,000 monks. Recent excavations confirm that the foundation of the stupa was 28 feet deep and rested on bedrock. This stupa, the tallest brick structure in the world, was built in keeping with engineering principles which are followed even today. At the time of the collapse of the Roman Empire, and counting this phase to be the end of the ancient world, this edifice was only second to two other taller structures - Pyramids 1 and 2 in Egypt, the taller of which was 483 feet.

The Samadhi Buddha, a limestone image, depicts the Buddha in a serene state of samadhi, or deep meditation.

The Jethawena stupa is the tallest brick structure in the world.

Kuttam Pokuna, or twin ponds, built in the 3rd century A.D. as a monks' bathing pool.

A careful examination of the Kuttam Pokuna, or twin ponds, reveals that one pond was smaller. Architecturally, they are regarded as masterpieces of that period. Their workmanship and symmetry are comparable to those of the best baths of the ancient world. The sensitivity with which these were designed is reflected in a framing shallow pool surrounding the two baths that retained a six-inch depth of water to cool off the feet before a dive into the greater depths.

MIHINTALE

Buddhism was introduced to Sri Lanka at Mihintale in 247 B.C. King Devanampiyatissa of Sri Lanka, who was on a hunting expedition, became a disciple of Buddha after the Buddhist missionary Mahinda preached a sermon. He was followed by his queen, his ministers, officials and the people. Mihintale thus became historically and religiously significant, and ever since it annually attracts pilgrims during the June full moon to commemorate the official introduction of Buddhism to Sri Lanka. To accomodate the lay and scholarly interest in Mihintale, both the sacred area and the town have undergone several phases of development, including a site museum. A rock inscription records the finest description of the running of a monastery in the 9th century A.D. It refers to the 200 or more serfs who assisted the religious congregation of 2,000. It also records the salaries paid to the physician, the surgeons, the teachers, potters, cooks and other workers. The lay assistants were instructed to submit the list of expenditures once a week, a summary of accounts at the end of each lunar month, and a balance sheet at the end of each year.

Refectory hall (left), stone inscriptions (above) and the relic chamber (below) at Mihintale where Buddhism was introduced to Sri Lanka by Prince Mahinda, the son of Indian Emperor Ashoka, in 247 B.C.

AUKANA

About 32 miles southeast of Anuradhapura can be found what is considered to be the finest statue of Buddha on the island. The name "Aukana" means "devourer of the sun": perfectly conserved, it is about 13 meters high and in recent times has been protected by a brick roofing. Dating to the 5th century, it is attributed to King Dhatusena.

Here, Buddha is represented standing, his right arm raised and his left arm bent over on his shoulder.

Sculpture in ancient Sri Lanka proposed numerous images of Buddha, who was generally depicted in three positions: seated with each foot resting on the opposite leg; again, seated with his arms crossed (Tivanka position); in a horizontal position.

In the latter it is the position of the feet which informs us if Buddha is sleeping (his toes are

Sculpted in the 5th century A.D., the 39-foot Aukana Buddha is best viewed at sunrise.

Bullock carts are a familiar sight on the road to Aukana.

joined together), or if he is entering Nirvana (his toes are slightly separated). Other differences in significance are indicated by the position of the hands (*mudra*): in the *dyana mudra*, both hands lie in his lap; in the *nvitarka mudra*, his index finger touches his thumb; in the *abhaya mudra*, his right hand is raised with the fingers joined together and the palm outstretched; in the *bumisparsa mudra*, his right hand is pointing downwards with his fingers extended.

The dry zone constitutes over a third of Sri Lanka. The area is scarcely populated and covers the northeast and portions of the northwest and southeast. Except for December through February, there is little rain, and water sources for man and agriculture are limited to the network of man-made reservoirs and a few rivers. However, the evergreen canopy of the jungle remains, and its wildlife continues to attract the visitor throughout the year.

Sri Lankan mud houses and bullock carts as a conveyance to ritualistic traditions and cultural practices, which are rare in the southwest quadrant, are found in this area. The ancient civilization which flourished in these areas for over one and a half millennia has now shifted to the wet zone in the southwest, but the remnants of the past stand testimony, enriching Sri Lanka's cultural heritage.

41

Parakrama Samudra, or the "sea of Parakrama", above, is a testament to Polonnaruwa's glorious past. Left, busy roadside markets in the heart of the ancient city.

POLONNARUWA

Polonnaruwa, the second capital, was the seat of government from the middle of the 11th century until the 13th century.

The Sinhala kingdom, subjected to constant invasions by Tamil armies from South India, was obliged to shift its capital to Dambadeniya. After the citadel was abandoned, it was rediscovered in the 19th century, and since the mid 1900's it has become a living city.

Unlike the ruins of Anuradhapura, which extended over an area of 16 square miles, the monuments of Polonnaruwa can be divided up into four zones. Both cities display an agrarian civilization, and the latter's original irrigation structures are unrivalled by any other contemporary culture. The Parakrama Samudra established by the hero king and great builder Parakramabahu I bears witness to the glories of the past.

This large irrigation reservoir, covering 5,940 acres, can irrigate 18,500 acres of rice paddies. On its banks is the Polonnaruwa Rest House, which at times has accommodated illustrious visitors including British royalty: among them, Queen Elizabeth II, in 1954. Interestingly, this was the Queen's first visit outside the British Isles after being crowned. A room at the rest house still holds an autographed portrait of the Queen and Prince Philip, a gift from the royal visitors.

A traveller to Polonnaruwa will often wonder about the identity of the image in front of the Parakrama Samudra. More recently, the Dutch scholar Kern has identified the controversial image, from a completely different set of iconographic details, as the deity Kappila, and has refuted its previous "identities" as a Sage or as a great King. Near the stone image is the Potgul Vihara, or Library shrine, one of the rare examples of domical brick building of the Polonnaruwa period. Even though the circular building has been interpreted, albeit without much scientific basis, as a library, it is now clear that the building was one of the satellite monasteries that existed during the reign of King Parakramabahu. If we count the excavated building units and compare this number with the texts, the Vihara complex could well have been the Kappila monastery described in the national chronicle, the Chulawamsa. The circular building is one of the rare examples of a domical brick building of the Polonnarawu period. A visit to the quadrangle, with its 12 structures, is a must for the visitor.

They include a two-storey building which once housed the sacred tooth relic. The stucco images around the building, some quite humourous, have survived.

A 12th-century statue, often referred to as "The Sage", but popularly believed to represent Parakramabahu I.

Remains of a building which houses the sacred Tooth Relic of the Buddha.

The foundation and the columns of the council chamber bear testimony to the reign of King Nissanka Malla, the last Polonnaruwa king to rule the whole of Sri Lanka. Most of the columns along the inner nave record the title of the minister who should sit alongside it. A special seat was provided to the right of the king, along the first column, for the Uva Raja or Deputy King. Nissanka Malla's throne, a masterpiece, has an ancient as well as recent history. In his search for fine objects, British Governor Gregory ordered that the lion throne of King Nissanka Malla be brought to the National Museum in Colombo. From Polonnaruwa to Matale it was rolled manually over timber logs by a team of workers, and was then sent by rail from Matale to Colombo. The Governor was so pleased that he sat on top of the lion and posed for a photograph. In 1964, respecting the museological regulation that artifacts should be kept as close as possible to the place of find, the lion throne was returned - on a low-bed trailer - to its pristine position.

Nissanka Malla's lion throne, left, and his council chamber, below, where the designations of the ministers and other officers who met in the chamber are carved on each pillar.

Ruins of Parakramabahu's seven-storey palace.

Parakramabahu's Palace is described in the Chulawamsa as a seven-storey edifice. The present brick walls show the grooves of the vertical timber columns and the wooden floors that rose up like a ziggurat, being reduced in area with each floor. The brick remains show the beginning of the 3rd floor, while the upper floors could well have been made out of timber. A grand stone stairway records the access that was provided to the upper floors. The lavatory stack, placed alongside the the building in the rear, was once the soil pit which carried the odours well beyond human contact. Surrounding the central buildings were the ground-floor out-buildings for storage and kitchens. Parakramabahu was not only a great builder, but also a military fig-ure - his reign included an attack on a South Indian State, and the captives were ordered to build a stupa, known as the Damila Maha Seya. This stupa, if completed during his reign, would have been the tallest monument in the world, reaching a height of 600 feet. An inscription confirms the king's military campaign and the foreign contacts which he main-tained at the time.

The royal baths, known as the Kumara pokuna, have a network of underground pipes connected to the Parakrama Samudra. Alongside the baths are the changing rooms and a pavilion probably meant for the elder royalty to watch the royal children bathe. The toilet unit attached to this edifice has an excellent drainage system. King Parkramabahu's achievements were numerous, from secular and religious building projects to an activist foreign policy similar to that practised by his predecessors. Parakramabahu's Council Chamber, a three-tiered structure supporting a wooden roof, would have appeared impressive. It is in the style of an open mandapa, but discreetly elevated to provide the privacy necessary for the royal council. The sculptures on each tier are objects of exceptional art and grace. The elephants, lions and dwarfs are all vigorously moving along, indicate the enjoyment that the sculptors had in their work.

Kumara Pokuna, or royal bath, of an intricate geometrical design, is fed by the Parakrama Samudra by means of underground stone conduits.

Paraakramabahu's council chamber with elaborate carvings of elephants and other animals around the base and the traditional moonstone and guard stones at the entrance.

Siva Devale, also called Vanam Madevi Isvaram, after the queen of Rajaraja I, the Chola conqueror who established his capital in Polonnaruwa.

The 7th-century Vatadage is believed to be the oldest monument in Polonnaruwa.

The Hindu shrines, 14 in all within the citadel and built by the Chola rulers of Polonnaruwa, have been restored. The Siva Devale No. 1, with a male lingam and a female yoni, is one of the finest Hindu temples of that period and houses stone sculptures of exceptional design. The shrine, that characteristically deviated from the standard Siva shrine plan in which an enclosed courtyard is found at the entrance to the temple, has an inner core which is substantially the standard Siva shrine design.

The Vatadage, or Circular Relic House, dating from the 7th century, was a part of a monastery which flourished in Polonnaruwa when the capital was still at Anuradhapura. The Vatadage has a stupa in the centre with four Buddha images facing the principal directions. Even though badly damaged, the images retain fine features, particularly in the headdress. The moonstone to welcome, and the guard stones to ward off evil, reflect the traditions of that time, and are of exceptional workmanship. Undoubtedly, the Vatadage had a wooden canopy, but today only the brick and the stone columns have survived.

The columns support a conical roof, as stated by recent scholars, although it was originally meant to have had a conical form. The architecture of the Vatadage is unique to Sri Lanka.

The Thuparama is the best-preserved building in Polonnaruwa.

Some of the 7th-century limestone images of the Buddha found within the Thuparama.

Thuparama is an image house meant for a colossal seated Buddha of brick and stucco. The brick edifice is vaulted in its interior and is the best-preserved example of vaulting in the country. The characteristics of the arch and vault in this edifice provide scientific details of a structural form that was special to South Asia. The limestone sculpture of the images found within the shrine dates to about the 7th century and distinctly reflects the early use of marble. The two large standing images are among the best in their class.

Lata Mandapa, an elaborate stupa house.

Atadage, the first Tooth Relic Shrine in Polonnaruwa, built by Vijayabahu I in the 11th century.

Lata Mandapa is the rococo of Sri Lanka, with flamboyancy at its extreme. The elegant pillars once supported a timber roof to house a small stupa which would have been used to exhibit the relics on special occasions for worship by the devotees. This 12th-century design probably replaced the more elaborate Vatadage type of stupa house, and evolved into another type of stupa house of the Gampola and Kandyan periods.

Atadage has the plan of an image house provided with a stone stairway leading to the upper floors where the sacred tooth relic was enshrined in the garbagruha. Some of the pillars at the shrine display relief sculpture, including a Buddha image, of a high quality. The Tamil inscription alongside is meant as a guideline to the Tamil guardians who were brought down from South India to protect the sacred relic, the palladium of sovereignty. This parallel of special guards brought in from abroad by the kings of the 12th century is internationally akin to that of the Swiss Guards who protect the Vatican.

Hatadage indicates a design parallel to Atadage's, where the ground floor housed the images and the upper floor retained the sacred tooth relic. Although the shrine proper is identical in size to Atadage, the edifice retains a bulky parapet surrounding the shrine. The battle for the sacred relic during the 12th century left a permanent stamp on the shrine where the images were badly damaged. The standing image in princely attire is that of a Bodhisatva figure. The image house has deteriorated badly. The Satmahalprasada, or seven-stepped stupa, can be seen in the distance beyond the second

Hatadage, or the second Tooth Relic Shrine, built in the 12th century.

A standing image in the princely attire of a Bodhisatva.

Gal Pota, or "Stone Book", which is eight metres long and 4.25 metres wide, bears inscriptions of Nissanka Malla's invasion of India and his relations with other countries.

Gal Vihara comprises the finest group of sculptures of the Buddha carved from a single granite wall.

The reclining image is 15 metres long.

tooth-relic shrine. The Gal Pota, or stone book, a carved and inscribed colossal piece of granite, is the work of King Nissanka Malla, who was fond of having himself praised by his poets. It has been suggested that some of the bards lavishly indulged in poetic licence.

The Gal Vihara is one of the finest groups of sculpture found anywhere in the world. It has been the site of worship for many millions of devotees. The recumbent figure, almost 50 feet in length, expresses a calmness of nirvana, symbolized in the plastic pliability of a human body very diligently cut out of hard granite. The standing figure, in a separate shrine, epitomizes calmness. This image depicts the rare mudra of *animisalochana*, where the Buddha is standing in front of the Bo tree in the seventh week after enlightenment to pay his personal respects to the tree for having provided shelter while he was meditating. (It is for this reason that a senior film director of a British television organization cited Buddha as being the first naturalist.) The delicately-sculpted figure protected in a cave has many decorative features of the *makara thorana*, or dragon entrance, and other Hindu deities flanking the image shrine. The seated figure even further in the distance expresses elegance, sublimity and awe that would command the attention and quiet of even noisy children.

Gal Vihara's two images of the seated Buddha in deep meditation. The image below is within an artificial cave, and is surrounded by various deities including Brahma and Vishnu.

Seven-metre-tall standing image of the Buddha in a rare cross-armed pose.

The inscription between the cave and the standing figure is one of the most important records of the Buddha sasana. It records the minutes of the extended meetings of the monks of the three chapters covering the extremes of Buddhism of Mahayana and Theravada (Hinayana). The king who provided the patronage for such a gathering ensured that the monks remained indoors until a final accord had been reached. It is this record that is indicated on the rock surface at Gal Vihara.

The journey from one ancient city to another passes through a picturesque terrain of pale green rice fields blending with the darker tones of the distant hills.

A traveller going from Polonnaruwa to Sigiriya or coming from Anuradhapura to Colombo will see hundreds of miles of paddy fields, rice being Sri Lanka's staple food. The ancient recognition given to rice by the early Sinhala kings is manifested in the hundreds of lakes and channels they created to irrigate this crop. Most of the old irrigation networks are still in use today. These waterways blend with the pale green of the rice fields and the darker green of the tree-clad hills, to make for some extremely picturesque scenery.

The Lion Rock of Sigiriya, the fortress-citadel of parricide king Kassapa, rises 600 feet above the surrounding scrub jungle.

SIGIRIYA

THE BATTLE OF SIGIRIYA

The story of the rock of Sigiriya is indissolubly linked to the tragic story of Kassapa and Moggallana, children of the same father, the King of Anuradhapura Dhatusena, but with different mothers. Moggallana's mother was in fact of royal blood. Although he was the elder, fearing that his step-brother would seize power, Kassapa took over the throne and imprisoned his father, while Moggallana succeeded in fleeing to India. After this, Kassapa ordered his father to reveal to him where the Crown treasure was hidden: the latter took him to the big Kalawewa dam which he himself had built and which he considered his most important work, and said to him: "This is where all my treasure is". Hearing this reply and feeling that he was being made fun of, Kassapa had his father immured.

In 495 the usurper king descended from the rock of Sigiriya in order to go and meet Moggallana who, strengthened by the support of the Chola and Sinhalese troops, had returned from India to engage his step-brother in battle on the plain surrounding Habarana. It was here that occurred the episode that decided the outcome of the battle: the elephant ridden by Kassapa scented the danger of a hidden bog and suddenly changed direction. Kassapa's army interpreted this action as a signal to retreat and dispersed, leaving the King alone. The King drew his dagger and cut his own throat.

The citadel of Sigiriya, founded 1,500 years ago by the parricide king Kassapa (447-495 A.D.), is one of the most remarkable creations in the world. The king transformed a 600-foot rock into an impregnable fortress, either to emulate Kuwera, the lord of wealth who resided upon Mount Alaka, or to counter the fear of a South Indian assisted army led by his brother Moggallana, the rightful heir to the throne, or both. Even though Sigiriya was inhabited before and after Kassapa, mostly by forest-dwelling monks, its surviving art and architecture are largely secular. Sigiriya was rediscovered after the rock was scaled by two Britishers in 1853, and since the mid 1900's the citadel has attracted millions of visitors from all around the world. Today, Sigiriya offers her visitors a gallery of 5th-century paintings cou-

pled with landscaped gardens unrivalled and unmatched by any contemporary citadel in the world. Paintings of 23 damsels, mostly in pairs and usually consisting of a lady and her maid, are found halfway up the rock. The maidens in the Sigiri murals have long been admired by both the art connoisseur and the average traveller. The graffiti inscribed on the mirror wall records the emotions of visitors touched by the beauty of Sigiriya. The beautiful maidens have received several interpretations. Based on Mahawansa, the national chronicle, as well as on other interpretations, the maidens in the Sigiri murals have been identified as the ladies in the court of Kassapa. They included his queens, daughters, maid servants and even concubines. The golden figures are shown in various profiles, some delicately holding a flower, others opening its petals or carrying a tray of flowers. Several hold their poses with seductive glances, turned-up lips, dropping shoulders, heavy bosoms, slender waists and arms. Their coiffures and detailed jewellery, clothes and make-up, not to mention their unsurpassing grace and beauty, immortalized by the Sigiri artists, continue to inspire generations of writers and poets.

The Mirror Wall owes its reflecting surface to an extraordinary coating of polished lime.

Some of the 23 Sigiriya maidens.

The maids, wearing transparent blouses, are darker in complexion than the bare-breasted royalty. Both categories are serene, gentle and cordial in their gestures. While their broad and tilted hips contrast with their narrow and taut waists, their full, rounded breasts bring out the most expressive feminine graces, features hitherto unexpressed in ancient classical art. Interpretations are numerous and poetic: the maidens are in the clouds, some gracefully gliding away towards the adjacent rock at Pidurangala to worship at the recumbent Buddha image, while others are waiting to greet the god King Kassapa.

More Sigiriya maidens.

Aerial view of the gardens and a platform.

At 600 feet, the view from the royal pavilions is arrestingly beautiful. The boulder and the pleasure gardens, admired for 1,500 years, reflect the skill and the technique of the early engineers. The principles used in the design of the gardens, as well as in the construction of both symmetric and asymmetric structures, speak highly for the art and architecture of 5th-century Sri Lanka. Archaeologists of this century have been generous in only excavating a part of this citadel. They have been prudent in leaving large areas un-excavated and not investigated, to be explored by future generations of scholars who will have even more advanced methods and finer techniques for studying the past.

Only the rock carving and the brick structure of the lion's mouth, through which millions of men, women and children have walked in order to admire and appreciate the citadel of the God King, have survived fires and the elements. The head of the lion has crumbled; but standing on the lion terrace, one could easily imagine how it might have looked during the Kassapa years.

The Lion Terrace leading to the summit.

The Royal Pavilion on the summit.

69

The Room of the Sigiriya Maidens.

The stairs to the Throne Hall and the Throne.

Sigiriya has become a goldmine for archaeologists and art historians. While stone was used at the basement and ground-floor levels, the upper-floor levels were all of tropical wood which was generally used for the construction of pavilions and other edifices. Only a few of the religious and secular monuments survive, but they continue to attract travellers from far and wide. Evidence of a sophisticated water system from the foot of Sigiriya to the summit, both for human consumption and for pleasure, has been found, and modern hydrologists continue to theorize on the accomplishments of the early engineers.

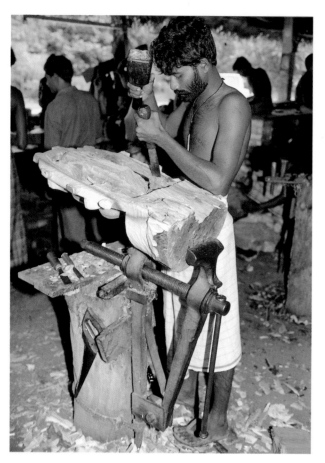

Craftsmen struggle to keep the traditional crafts of wood carving and sculpture alive.

Sri Lankan craftsmen within the cultural triangle of Anuradhapura, Polonnaruwa and Kandy, continue to emulate the products of their forefathers. Some of the wood carvings, stone images and ceramic ornaments closely resemble the originals of the masters deposited in the older temples and residences. While some craftsmen still employ the techniques used by their predecessors, a few apply new technology in making these art objects. These reproductions, as well as a few originals, are sold to the visitor at bargain prices, often outside historic and religious sites.

DAMBULLA

Dambulla is reminiscent of the past. For many centuries, the surroundings of Dambulla, an area of over fifty acres, was the habitation of forest-dwelling monks. While these had minimal contact with the public, meditation was their main strength. Archaeological data confirm that the cave shrines of Dambulla, renowned as the temple of the infinite Buddhas, was a place of religious worship when the capital was at Anuradhapura. According to extant inscriptions, the caves in the shrine as well as in the surroundings were donated to the monks by royalty, nobility, monks and nuns. More recently, the climb to the cave shrine, 600 feet above the plains and 100 feet above sea level, has been made easier.

Scrub jungle surrounding the Dambulla cave temple.

Exterior views of the Dambulla temple.

The principal shrine at Dambulla, known as the Rangiri Dambulu Viharaya, or the golden cave temple of Dambulla, has been cited in a number of religious and historical texts. As a visitor enters the shrine, there is a 25-line 12th-century inscription of King Nissanka Malla of Polonnaruwa, who took credit for the construction of images of the Buddha and for conducting a religious service. Similarly, other rulers have patronized the shrine since pre-Christian times up to the 18th century. The façade is more recent: it was constructed in 1938. The paintings in the temples are the work of several hundred artists spanning a number of generations. The images in a number of postures are those of the Buddha, the bodhisatvas, gods and goddesses, monks, disciples and kings. Covering 25,000 square feet, the area of paintings in the shrine is the largest in South Asia and the oldest in the world.

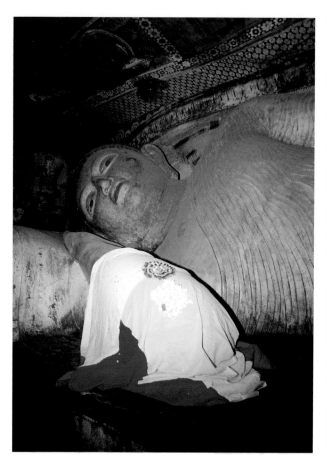

Some of the numerous images of the Buddha inside the first and second cave temples.

The elaborate ceiling paintings follow the natural folds of the rock so that some visitors mistake it for cloth.

The Rangiri Dambulu Viharaya has five temples. The first temple has seven images - the Buddha passing away, his disciple Ananda, Vishnu and four other Buddhas. Vishnu is lord of the gods in the Hindu pantheon, but is also worshipped by the Buddhists. The second temple has sixty images of the Buddha, Naatha bodhisatva, Maitriya bodhisatva, God Upulvan, God Saman and King Valaagamba and King Nissanka Malla. This impressive cave has several significant paintings on its ceiling - the life of the Buddha, enlightenment of the Buddha, the migration of Vijaya, the official intro-

duction of Buddhism, the planting of the Bo tree, the wars against the invaders, etc. A geological flaw in the formation of the rock, where two molten bubbles meet, has created a tiny space where water seeps into the cave and drops into a bowl. With time it has acquired sanctity, religious and ritualistic interest, the water being used for various religious functions. The ancient artists appreciated the drip from an aesthetic point of view, and provided a staggered panel following the fissure with the design of stream in which large fish are seen floating in the plastered surroundings.

Images in the second temple.

Images in the third, fourth and fifth temples are on pages 80 and 81.

The third temple, built by a Kandyan king on the advice of a monk, has a 30-foot reclining image which separates it from the fourth temple. This temple also has over 50 standing and seated images of the Buddha, as well as a life-size image of the king. The fourth temple, small but unique, contains several images of the Buddha and a miniature stupa. The fifth temple is the most recent and has a reclining Buddha surrounded by a number of Buddhist images. This temple also houses images of Kataragama, a Buddhist god, Devata Bandara, a local god and Vishnu, the god who alleviates the sufferings of the people.

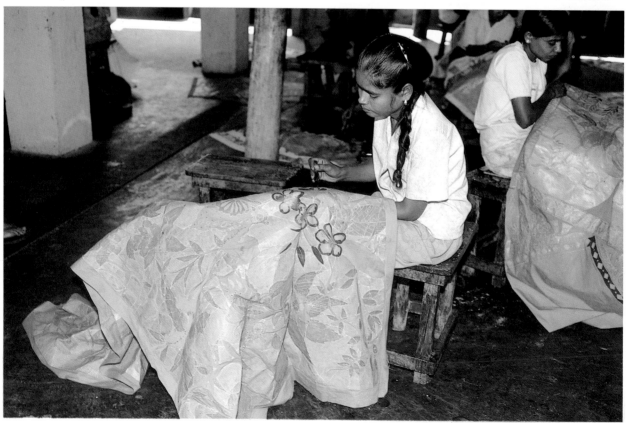

THE WORKING OF BATIK

It is certain that no tourist leaves Sri Lanka without having purchased some batik, the island's traditional fabric. The working of batik, that is made in the most varied and refined designs and colours, is extremely interesting and is willingly shown to the tourists. A design is made on the originally white fabric. Then, a layer of wax is poured through a fine funnel onto the part that is to be coloured in a certain tonality. The fabric is then dried and washed; the first layer of wax is removed from it and a second one is applied, once again leaving free the part intended to receive another colour. The procedure is always repeated in this way, with successive applications of wax, colour and washings, until the fabric is obtained complete with all its colours on the design. Obviously, batiks of large dimensions and complex designs need a longer work period: in certain cases, this lasts months and months.

Women making colourful batik designs.

Roadside vendors add colour to the village landscape.

Hindu temple architecture in Sri Lanka, in many ways unique in the original Indian styles and designs, has become a major area of study. Perhaps this is the result of the infusion of Hinduism with Buddhism to produce works of religious art, or the early introduction of Hinduism from the subcontinent and its development with limited influence from the mainland. In Sri Lanka, Hinduism is the second largest denomination after Buddhism. Most Hindus live in the northeast of Sri Lanka or in the Central Province. In the Western Province, the largest concentrations of Hindus are in Wellawatte and Kotahena. However, there are Hindu shrines in most Buddhist temples. Hindu devotees fundamentally worship the Trinity - Brahma the creator, Vishnu the preserver, and Shiva the destroyer - and thousands of other gods and goddesses in the Hindu pantheon.

Elaborate imagery characterizes the façades of Hindu temples.

Kandy, one of the most beautiful cities in the world.

KANDY

Kandy, Sri Lanka's cultural capital, is one of the most beautiful cities in the world. This capital, founded by Vimaladharmasurya I in 1592, was the seat of government during the Dutch and Portuguese occupations of the maritime provinces and until British rule in 1815.

The valley of Kandy, surrounded by inaccessible hills, was in many ways the last bastion of the Sinhalese, until Sri Wickrama Rajasinghe, the last monarch of Sri Lanka, was captured by the British with the assistance of Sinhala nobles who were disgruntled with his irrational decisions. History records that the King was turned into an alcoholic by his foreign enemies.

Some of the decisions that he made were paranoid, such as the impaling of over 100 advisors on the reservoir bund of a paddy field because they had advised him against converting the paddy field into a lake. The King, who was a great admirer of beauty and landscapes, had the paddy field dredged into the present Kandy lake and the bund into an island before he was captured and exiled to Mauritius.

Even though Kandy is a relatively new city, there is scattered evidence to point to its having been inhabited at least 800 years ago. The Royal Palace now has an inscription referring to King Nissanka Malla of Polonnaruwa, who visited the site in the 12th century. Today, Kandy offers the visitor a rich collection of temples and ancient houses, traditional handicrafts and souvenirs, and cultural practices and rituals.

There is an annual pageant in Kandy: elephant bathing, boating on the lake, the Botanical Gardens, the water falls and the mountains are only some of the attractions.

The Dalada Maligawa, or Temple of the Tooth Relic of the Buddha, is Kandy's main attraction.

Since the sacred tooth relic of the Buddha was brought to the island, it has remained with royalty. The relic was enshrined in Kandy in a building that Vimmaladharmasurya I, the founder of the capital, had constructed; it was subsequently placed by his successors in new and renovated buildings.

The temple known as the Dalada Maligawa has undergone several phases of development, including the incorporation of a Pathirippuwa, or octagon, which now houses a rare collection of Buddhist books.

The custodian of the Temple of the Sacred Tooth, the Diyawadana Nilame, ensures the smooth functioning of the temple.

The entrance to the temple is over the moat, and a stone stairway leads the visitor through a tunnel to the drummers' courtyard. Facing the visitor is a two-storey building the upper floor of which enshrines the gem-studded gold caskets containing the sacred tooth relic of the Buddha. Millions of devotees have venerated the sacred relic. Through the ages, thousands of other objects, made mostly out of precious stones and metals and donated to the temple by rulers, dignitaries and well-wishers, have come to adorn the sacred chamber. Every day thousands of devotees gather at this sacred temple from throughout Sri Lanka to light lamps, offer incense and pay homage to the Enlightened One whose sacred tooth relic is enshrined there. The monks, as well as those in attendance, including drummers, perform their daily rituals. The art, architecture and paintings in the temple, stand testimony to the generosity of the King and other members of royalty who patronized the temple through the years to enhance its beauty and enrich its history.

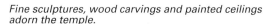

Fine sculptures, wood carvings and painted ceilings adorn the temple.

The Natha Devale, one of the four Hindu and Buddhist shrines in the proximity of the Temple of the Tooth Relic, dates to the 14th century. The devale has been restored to its original design. The image in the devale is that of Avalokitesswara Natha, a previous life of the Buddha. Before consecration, all kings were obliged to worship at the devale and choose their royal name in front of the image. The view of the Dalada Maligawa across the lake has often captured the imagination of the traveller. At the other end is the Queens, a hotel associated with British royalty and which still retains some of the old architectural styles. The lake offers boat rides, and a park at the other extremity provides a playground for children.

The **Nuwara Perahera**, or Pageant of Kandy, is the most colourful procession in the world. About 100 caprisoned elephants and over 100 dancers, drummers and noblemen, led by the custodian of the Temple of the Sacred Tooth Relic, parade past hundreds of thousands of spectators while these pay homage to the sacred tooth relic enshrined in a golden casket carried by the Raja Aliya, or King of the Elephants. In keeping with the tradition established at Anuradhapura, the procession moves along the street for seven consecutive nights and concludes on the day of the August full moon.

The Natha Devale, the oldest building in Kandy.

The Kandy Lake, a 19th-century creation of Kandy's last king, Sri Wickrama Rajasinha.

TRADITIONAL DANCES

In Sri Lanka, as moreover in most of the Orient, dance is the instrument for narrating stories that belong to the Sinhalese cultural patrimony. Two styles of dance exist on the island: the dance of the lowlands (typical of the coastal strip south of Colombo) and the dance of the highlands, known above all as the Kandy school. In turn, the latter experiences two types of representation: the more spectacular one of a warlike nature, dynamic and acrobatic, and the one belonging to the magic rituals, performed by witch doctors, but that can rarely be seen. The dance is always accompanied by monochordal music, the typical instrument for which is the drum (twenty-six varieties of drums exist in Sri Lanka), to which is united the sound of the cymbal, flute, oboe, and sometimes shells, etc. The costumes worn by the dancers are rich in decorations and jewels. The men have their chests, backs and hips covered with silver plates and wear a headdress also of silver and hung with charms and pendants that jingle at the slightest movement. In the "devil's dance", instead, the dancers wear the typical painted wooden mask. The women, wrapped in multi-coloured fabrics, wear magnificent headdresses and bracelets with bells on both their wrists and ankles.

A moment of the "Maname Katava" dance, a twentieth-century Sinhalese work inspired by the popular Buddhist tales called "Jataka" (below left).

A Kandyan dancer (above). A devil dancer (below right).

NATIONAL MUSEUM

The National Museum in Kandy displays some of the finest objects of art from the 16th century to the 19th century. The Museum houses the largest collection of Buddha statues of the Kandyan period, characterized by a Buddha with a flame over his head and wearing the characteristic wavy robe. The crown, the images of the nobles, and the wooden carvings preserved in the Museum are the finest examples of the Gampola and Kandyan periods.

Some of the fine displays at the National Museum in Kandy.

ROYAL BOTANICAL GARDENS

The Royal Botanical Gardens are among the finest tropical gardens in the world. They have a comprehensive collection and a scientific programme in biotechnology, ecology, conservation and taxonomy. The history of the gardens dates to 1371, when royalty shifted their court to Peradeniya and, subsequently, when King Kirthi Sri Rajasinghe (1747-1780) made them into royal gardens. Their modern history started when a garden named Kew was started at Slave Island in Colombo, and then shifted to Kalutara for reasons of more space, and thereafter to Peradeniya in 1821 by Alexander Moon. The gardens, open every day, have flowers in bloom throughout the year. To mark their visits to Sri Lanka, many distinguished visitors - from royalty to Heads of State and Government - have planted trees at the Gardens. Today, these gardens have acquired a worldwide reputation, both for their history and for their plant collection.

About 4,000 plant species thrive in the Royal Botanical Gardens in Peradeniya.

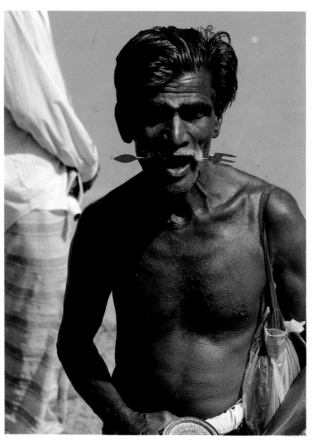

Sri Lanka is rich in astrologers, soothsayers and religious people who share their knowledge with the enthusiastic visitor. For some it has become a commercial venture, but for others the art and science of the occult come first. Similarly, there are snake charmers and others from old gypsy bands who travel throughout the country, practising their ancient trade and entertaining interested passersby.

A Hindu devotee has his cheeks pierced to fulfil a vow.

A snake charmer at work.

A giant tusker feeds while a mahout, or trainer, leads his mate to cool off in the river.

Today, the **Sri Lankan elephant**, estimated between 2,500 and 3,000 in number, is endangered. At the turn of the century, the elephant population was assessed at 20,000 animals. The Sri Lankan elephant is more trainable than the African species and can be easily domesticated. The elephants baths at Katugastota and Mawanella have been a major attraction for some time. After working for about half the day, the elephants are watered or allowed to lie in shallow water to cool off and recuperate from their heavy work. On request, visitors are taken for a ride on the elephant, and some are picked up by the animal in its trunk. The most theatrical sight to be photographed is an elephant holding the mahout in his mouth or spurting water at the visitors.

NUWARA ELIYA

Nuwara Eliya, known as the garden city of Asia for its hills, valleys and waterfalls, is 6,182 feet above sea level and is situated at the foot of Mount Pidurutalagala, Sri Lanka's highest peak. Nuwara Eliya was discovered in 1819 by Sir Samuel Baker, the famous explorer who discovered the source of the Nile. Thereafter, an English village was established, the remains of which can still be seen. The colonial government habitually moved to Nuwara Eliya for 3 months of the year: March, April and May, when Colombo was warm and humid. Since then, thousands of domestic and foreign tourists sojourn in Nuwara Eliya, to relish the salubrious climate, play golf, enjoy the park, admire the high-grown tea plantations, visit the Hakgala gardens and travel to Worlds End at Horton Plains, where there is a sudden drop in the terrain of several thousand feet. The Grand Hotel and the Hill Club are the finest in Nuwara Eliya, and their more recent architecture continues to be admired by holidaymakers.

Velvety carpets of tea plants spread over the hills of Nuwara Eliya.

HARVESTING THE TEA LEAVES

A Japanese legend narrates how one day, in order to stay awake to meditate, Buddha tore out his eyelashes. In falling, these miraculously caused the birth from the soil of two luxuriant green tea plants. Much more realistically, the tea plant - which today is the first item in the Sri Lankan economy - is the *Camelia Sinensis*, a robust evergreen which, for the sake of convenience in harvesting it, is kept cut low like a shrub. The leaves are oblong and dentate, reaching a length of up to 10 centimeters; the flower has five white petals, and the fruit is shaped like a capsule. The tea plant is cultivated at three levels of altitude: from sea level up to 600 meters (low grown), from 600 to 1200 meters (mid grown), and higher than 1200 meters (high grown). Its harvest is begun starting from the third year of the plant's life. Traditionally, it is the women who harvest the tea, picking together two leaves and a bud known as a *pekoe*. At this point the leaves are immediately taken to the factory, where the real workmanship begins. The first phase is the *drying*, during which the leaves are spread out for 18 hours over nylon nets that are assailed from below with a flow of warm air. The next step is the *rolling*, in which the leaves are broken up by means of a special metal roller. The next step is the crucial one in the working: the *fermentation*, which takes place in a cold, ventilated room where, by means of enzyme action, the tea is made to ferment by oxydyzing the tannin of the leaves. The procedure lasts for about two hours, and it is at this point that the tea assumes its characteristics. The following phase is the *baking*, which halts the fermentation process and lowers the humidity of the leaves from 65% to 2%. The final phase is the *selection*, during which the leaves are sifted and separated according to the different characteristics. The best quality obtained is the Broken Orange Pekoe (B.O.P.). At this point the tea is packaged and put up for sale, the latter being directly controlled by the Tea Board that is part of the Sri Lankan Ministry for Industry and Commerce. By law, tea auctions are held in Colombo; but, with the Tea Board's permission, a producer can also send his harvest to London.

A bevy of industrious tea pluckers carefully pick the first two leaves and bud off each stem.

The leaves picked from the fields are sorted and processed in factories to produce some of the best tea in the world.

A worker taps the sap from a rubber tree.

THE RUBBER INDUSTRY

Perhaps only a few people know that here in Sri Lanka are located the oldest rubber plantations in the world. Just like tea, rubber is one of the most important items in the country's economy. Rubber is obtained from the rubber tree (*Hevea brasiliensis*) by making an oblique cut in the bark and collecting in a container (usually a coconut shell) held under the cut the laticiferous juice that comes out. Every two or three days for ten months, the cut is lengthened by approximately one millimeter. During the other two months, the trees lose their leaves and so the operation is suspended. The juice is called "latex" and once it has been gathered in buckets, it is taken to the factory. Here, it is filtered and "standardized" (that is, water is added) and is placed in recipients in which it will solidify. It is then passed through rollers that reduce it to sheets of the desired thickness. These sheets are hung up in warming chambers, in order to facilitate the drying; lastly, they are sold.

The tall images at Buduruwagala.

The spectacular Ella Gap Falls.

At Ella, 12 miles south of Badulla, are the spectacular Ravana Ella Falls, 27 feet in height, and the Ella Gap from which point the terrain drops by 3,000 feet.

Between Ella and Hambanthota is Wellawaya. Three miles south of Wellawaya is Buduruwagala, where seven colossal images, partly carved into the living rock and partly worked out in plaster, persuade the visitor to take a brief detour. The traces of paint examined to date confirm that the images were painted. These Mahayana (and not the traditional Theravada (Hinayana)) images date from the 8th to the 10th centuries A.D. Controversy surrounds the identification of the two groups of images flanked by the 51-foot central image of the Buddha, the tallest in Sri Lanka. While the images to the right of the Buddha are of Avalokiteswara accompanied by his consort Tara and a Bodhisatva, the images to the left are of Manjusri accompanied by two other Bodhisatvas.

Wildlife abounds at Bundala National Park, particularly a large herd of wild elephants.

BUNDALA NATIONAL PARK

The Bundala National Park is the most recent park in Sri Lanka to be declared a wildlife and nature reserve. The other, better-known parks are in Yala Wilpattu, Uda Walawe, Randenigala, Wasgamuwa, Somavathiya, Maduru Oya and in the Flood Plains. Bundala sits in a salt pan surrounded by thick jungle, and is about half an hour's journey from Hambanthota. The flora and fauna in the park range from macaques to water buffalo and the gray langer. The park is also famous for its non-aggressive but wild elephants and its flamingos. During the migratory season of October through April, the flamingos fly thousands of miles to Bundala to feed on the molluscs and crustacea in the salt pan.

Left, boats and fishermen take a break before going out to sea.

Above, a typical fishing hut.

TANGALLE

The southern town of Tangalle, 110 miles from the city of Colombo, offers to the visitor the enticing blend of a Sri Lankan village and coastal living. The people, their life styles and their customs are all shaped by a calm and quiet way of living. Tangalle's four-mile-wide bay, sheltered by an off-shore reef, is popular with swimmers and offers skin divers some spectacular underwater sights.

Galle's picturesque harbour.

The New Oriental Hotel is not new - it was built in 1684 as a barracks for Dutch troops.

The Dutch Reform Church.

GALLE

Galle was a port of call for foreign fleets from the Chinese armadas of Cheng Ho in the 1400's and for the Dutch and British, who all left their indelible imprint on the Galle Fort and its surrounding ramparts. On the skyline are a prominent lighthouse, a mosque of rare design, and several early buildings, now conserved and restored and in use both as government offices and as residences. The backdrop is the old harbour, where a diver can find artifacts, from Persian potsherds to Chinese celadon and Dutch ceramics. The New Oriental Hotel, built by the Dutch in 1684 as their barracks, was converted into a hotel by the British in 1845. Today, the hotel is one of the oldest in Sri Lanka and has all the characteristics of the last phase of the Dutch occupation of Sri Lanka and the beginning of the British period.

What is unique in the art and architecture of this building is its Dutch scale. However, the arch windows and rain shelters are British in style, and its completion during the British period is clearly stamped as the work of two distinct builders. The Dutch design of massive halls and lavish timber beams, Dutch plates and bowls, and the Dutch owners and menu take the visitor back, at least briefly, to 18th-century Holland.

Next-door is the Dutch Reform Church, one of the finest religious monuments surviving from the Dutch period. Its gravestone inscriptions, mostly in memory of Europeans and describing men, women and children who were lost at sea or families that died of illness or at the hands of pirates, are extremely moving.

Galle remains archaic but cosmopolitan: ramparts from the Portuguese period complement Dutch and British architecture, along with Muslim mosques and other modern structures.

Even today Galle is a port of call for hundreds of modern vessels, reminiscent of a yesteryear when sailing vessels of the Dutch Vereenigde Oost Indische Compagnie (VOC) and ships of the British East India Company frequented this southernmost port of the subcontinent. Today, the fort has a National Maritime Museum and a National Museum, both displaying the country's heritage, with emphasis on the maritime regions and colonial collections. With Dutch assistance, a special programme is under way to conserve and restore the ramparts, the buildings and the other monuments in the fort. The mosque has adopted a façade of neo-renaissance character with Mogul motifs incorporated into the design detail. Of all the colonial forts in Asia, the Galle fort has a truly impressive history and is rich in its colonial architecture. There are several colonial houses, many of them well maintained, in this vicinity. Their art and architecture are that of one hundred years ago in Sri Lanka, when wooden decorations were characteristic. The fretwork type of decorations that line the eaves and act as glare-breaker at eye level, expresses a feature that was familiar to such house constructions. Houses with a blend of traditional workmanship and European styles of the past are rare but extant.

WELIGAMA

Weligama, about 85 miles from Colombo, is a coastal town. Its attractions are many, from ancient shrines to stilt fishing. Stilt fishing, when the fishermen are supported by wooden poles standing in the shallow ocean, has captivated many poets and travellers. A rare form of night fishing, it has its origins in South Asia, and is inexpensive. This form of fishing is mostly confined to the shallow bays and coves, and involves using a spedal bait to catch small fish.

Other views of Galle's ramparts.

Weligama, famous for its stilt fishing and rose-red ironstone cliffs.

Madel fishing, or shore seining, at Kalutara, while below right, a fishing boat goes out to sea to lay the nets for the next day's catch.

KALUTARA

Kalutara is well-known for its traditional seagoing vessels and indigenous fishing methods, such as madel fishing or shore seining. The 10 main types and 60 sub-types of traditional crafts have attracted scholars, starting with James Hornell in the 1940's to Gehard Kapitan and Eric Kentley more recently. The introduction of fibreglass boats, mechanization and motorization since the 1960's have replaced over 40% of the traditional fleet.

The Kalutara Bodhiya, or stupa at Kalutara, has been designed as a modern concrete version of the old Vatadage, the Circular Relic Shrine, and is a stupa within a hollow exterior stupa. Buddha images are placed around the inner stupa facing in the four cardinal directions. The calm of the interior is often disturbed by the reverberations from a domical whispering gallery.

Roadside fish markets at the small fishing town of
Kosgoda. Its wide stretches of unspoilt beaches attract
mating turtles.

Overleaf, fishing boats on the beaches of Kosgoda.

Pages 120-123: charming views of the beaches
along the coast

KOSGODA

Kosgoda is another coastal town, and is best known
for its fishing activity. Mud houses with thatched
roofs and traditional water craft are seen throughout its coast. Annually, its wide beaches and serene
surroundings attract thousands of visitors. Many of
them enjoy a ride on an outrigger catamaran, and
they also visit the turtle hatchery, established for the
purpose of conserving this endangered species.

A giant hollow stupa, housing a smaller stupa and images of the Buddha, stands on the banks of the Kaluganga and serves as a major landmark.

Rags-to-riches stories abound in the gem pits of Ratnapura.

RATNAPURA

For centuries Sri Lanka has been known as the land of gems, and is said to have the highest concentration of gem-bearing material in the world. Although more than 50 varieties of gemstones are mined from Sri Lanka's gem gravel, the country is most famous for its blue sapphires, chrysoberyl cat's eyes and, more recently, for unusual orange-pink sapphires known as padmaraga that are found only in Sri Lanka. Among other varieties found in the gem-bearing gravel called illam are a range of colours of sapphires and star sapphires, alexandrite, aqua-marines, topaz, garnets, blue and white moonstones, amethysts and a host of other gemstones belonging to the quartz family.

Since King Solomon sent his emissaries to Ceylon to procure wonderful gems to woo the elusive Queen of Sheba, royalty and the rich and famous throughout the world have followed suit. The 400-carat blue sapphire called "Blue Belle" which adorns the British crown is from Sri Lanka, and so is the beautiful blue star sapphire mis-named the "Star of India"

A traditional pit mine in Ratnapura.

Illam, the coarse gem-bearing gravel, dug up from the mines, is swirled through water in cane baskets and then sorted by keen- eyed miners who can easily spot a ruby, sapphire or cat's eye.

which is on permanent display at the Museum of Natural History in New York.

Sri Lanka's gem deposits are mainly alluvial, washed down from their original mountain locations into river beds and valleys. The most important gem-bearing area is Ratnapura - City of Gems - and its environs.

To reach the gem-bearing illam, which is often covered by layers of alluvial clay, workers dig pits and support the walls with logs or planks. Once the illam is hoisted out of the pits, it is swirled through water in basket-like sieves so that the clay is washed away. Keen-eyed workers then hand-pick the gem material, which is cut and polished into sparkling gems at factories in and around Ratnapura and Colombo. Recently, Sri Lanka has become a major producer of small, well-cut, calibrated stones which are in great demand worldwide in the jewellery-manufacturing industry.

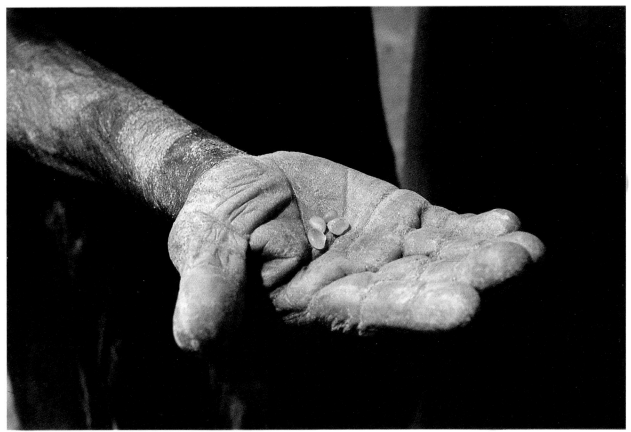

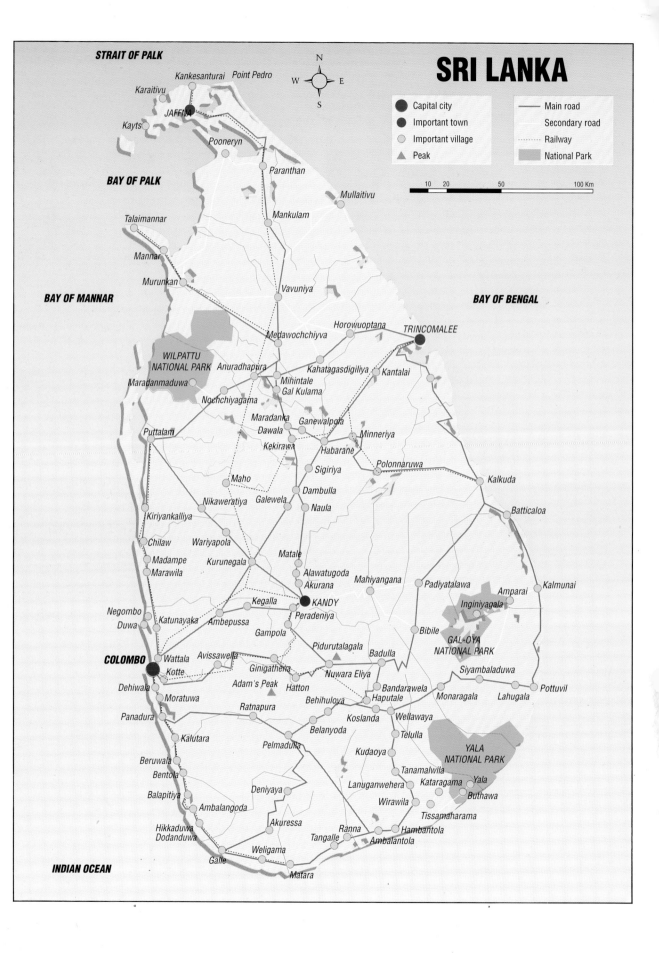